114

811.6 Swe

Poems about myself by America's
children.

Poems About
MYSELF

BY America's Children

EDITED BY Jacqueline Sweeney

BENCHMARK BOOKS

MARSHALL CAVENDISH
NEW YORK

For ALL the children—you've been my teachers and will always be my heart. J.S.

The publisher and editor would like to thank the following schools for opening their doors to us: Alden Place and Elm Drive Elementary Schools (Millbrook Central School District), Amenia and Millerton Elementary Schools (Webutuck School District), Barnum Woods Elementary School (East Meadow Union Free School District), Beekman, LaGrange, and Noxon Road Elementary Schools (Arlington Central School District), Boght Hills and Blue Creek Elementary Schools (North Colonie Central School District), Carrie E. Tompkins Elementary School (Croton-Harmon School District), Central Avenue Elementary School (Mamaroneck Union Free School District), Gardnertown Fundamental Magnet School (Newburgh Enlarged City School District), Germantown Central School (Germantown Central School District), Hackley School, Pawling Elementary and Middle Schools (Pawling Central School District), Scotchtown Avenue School (Goshen Central School District), Tesago Elementary School (Shenendehowa Central School District)

Special thanks to: Miriam Arroyo, Barbara Bortle, Ellen Brooks, Angela Butler, Pat Conques, Dotti Griffin, Anahid Hamparian, Peggy Hansen, Sandy Harvilchuck, Naomi Hill, Carol Ann Jason, Jennifer Lombardo, Mary Lynne Oresen, Joanne Padow, Carol Patterson, Theresa Prairie, Tracy Racicot, Ellen Ramey, Linda Roy, Nicole Sawotka, Jude Smith, Faye Spielberger, Bev Strong, John Szakmary, Glen White, Mary Ellen Whitely

Benchmark Books
Marshall Cavendish
99 White Plains Road
Tarrytown, NY 10591-9001
www.marshallcavendish.com

Text copyright © 2003 by Jacqueline Sweeney
Illustrations copyright © 2003 by Marshall Cavendish Corporation

Book design by Anahid Hamparian

Library of Congress Cataloging-in-Publication Data
Poems about myself by America's children / edited by Jacqueline Sweeney.

   p. cm. -- (Kids express)
Summary: Poetry and art by elementary school children about how they perceive themselves and the world around them.
  ISBN 0-7614-1504-1
  1. Self--Juvenile poetry. 2. Children's poetry, American. 3.
Children's writings, American. [1. Self-perception--Poetry. 2. American
poetry. 3. Children's writings. 4. Children's art.] I. Sweeney,
Jacqueline. II. Series.
  PS595.S45 P64 2002
  811'.60809282--dc21

                          2002002190

Printed in Hong Kong
6   5   4   3   2   1

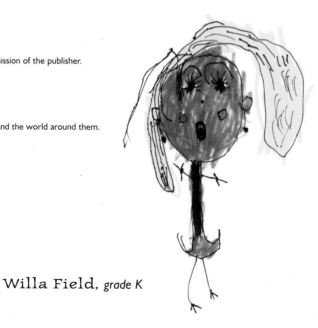

Willa Field, *grade K*

Contents

Teacher's Note

Imagine a classroom full of elementary school children bursting into applause upon hearing an announcement of an upcoming activity. Recess? Lunch? No. Writing poetry! Year after year, this is Jackie Sweeney's effect on students. I have been fortunate enough to witness this phenomenon over the last six years, as Jackie has conducted poetry residencies in the Arlington Central School District.

I study her as she teaches, trying to analyze her strategies. Although I have learned a lot from doing so, there is also some kind of magic at work here. Jackie is a modern-day alchemist, helping students turn their writing into something quite extraordinary.

What does she do? First, she convinces students that they are safe and their ideas are exciting. She focuses on free verse, providing structures through which she introduces students to poetic techniques such as sensory imagery, simile, metaphor, personification, and diction. At the same time, she invites students to surprise her with their own interpretations of these structures. She models extensively with examples from her own imagination and from the work of other students. Her samples are carefully chosen to counteract the notion that poetry treats only butterfly wings and flowers; topics range over every possible subject, from slithering pythons to pestering siblings.

Sensory perceptions are combined in surprising ways. Jackie might begin by asking students to picture a certain color and let it make them feel cold or hot or cool or warm. This is quickly developed into simile as she asks the students to consider how the color (let's say "red") is hot "like what"? As the students come up with their first tentative similes, Jackie immediately gets them to elaborate by asking questions until the child has produced: "Red makes me feel hot like a tomato on a white plate on a picnic table with the sun beating down on it on a summer day." Jackie exclaims, "Now I can see it!" and we are off on another year's excursion into poetry.

Peggy C. Hansen
Noxon Road Elementary School
Poughkeepsie, New York

Changing Things

The Most amazing thing I have ever
known is the way things change.
One minute there could be a sparkling
sun and the next it could be
gloomy and gray. Sometimes, when
things change too fast I feel like
I'm spinning all around in an
airless room. You can love and you
can hate. Changes sometimes creep in
slowly but others rip through the air.
It amazes me how much I change.
I grow taller and smarter. Some changes
are good like growing but some
changes are bad like dying. When
I get yelled at when I am loud, I
want to change my ways by being quiet.
One thing that will never change
is how wondrous I feel inside.

—Jessica, *grade 5*

—Julianna Tangredi, *grade 4*

I Don't Wish

I don't wish I was a frog. I
don't wish I was a bird. I
don't wish I was a lizard. I
just wish I was me—plain
old me.

—James Vogel, *grade 5*

Me

I am a short stubborn kid who
doesn't listen. I am an angel and
I always listen. I am both
mixed like you.

—Jennifer Wild, *grade 4*

Crazy

I feel crazy every day. I feel like
a big fat lemon squeezing out my
juice. I feel like I can't stop like
I can't even move. I hear screeching
all around. I feel like I'm bright bright
orange. It feels like thunder crashing
through my head. I drive my dog crazy
when I'm jumping all around. I feel
like a big baboon jumping in the trees
snakes trying to bite in the hot sun.
It drives me crazy every day. Sometimes
I just calm down and play with my
dog and then watch some T.V.

—Cody Broast, *grade 2*

—Nicole Esoff, *grade 2*

Very Hyper

I ran 20 miles per hour. I got very
tired. I went 10 miles on my scooter. My
wheels got very dirty. I'm very hungry.
And feel good. I think I'm special.
I went on a skating ramp with my friends.
I went too high. My skates flew off. I
landed on a rock. My skates landed
on the roof. It did not bother me that
I did that. I felt very happy.
I think I need smaller skates.

—Michael Gorey, *grade 2*

Kaboom Balloon

When I'm hyper
I feel like a wild
balloon on the loose flying high to
the sky with a tiny boy chasing me.
I feel like a bright green tree.
Hyper is like wild animals.
Perhaps one day I will pop.
　　　KABOOM!

—Mitchell Bernstein, *grade 2*

—Aaron Konigsberg, *grade 4*

Color Blind

I feel good and bad about my colors. I can see some colors and the grass is green but I see it orange. Pink is like red hot peppers and I feel good and bad about colors.

A lot of people ask me what color is this and that. That is fine that they ask me what colors are because they don't know what colors I see. That is how I am. Color blind. I feel bad because I want to see what other people see in the world.

—Mike Major, *grade 5*

—Tyler Bello, *grade 2*

9

When I'm happy I feel like

light rain hitting the grass lightly
and it feels like I'm in a soft
bed resting. And then someone
walks into my mind
and I feel like that person is
trying to tell me something
about this side of my mind
like there's something special
there. It makes me feel like
I can see that special thing in
my mind a little but there is
something blocking the way
in my mind and it's black
and makes me feel sad—
because I really want to
see this thing and there's
a thing blocking the way.
Can you help me
get past this thing?

—Alexander Reminick, *grade 2*

Clam

There's a clam in me that holds
all my private thoughts for me like
a chest full of gold with
no key.

—Sam W., *grade 4*

—Dylan Henschel, *grade 3*

My Guitar

The wind is as cold as winter
when I play my guitar.
As the wind blows my guitar
keeps singing.
The music keeps going as the
wind keeps going and
will never stop!
Because the music is in
my heart and it will stay there
in my heart.
I just wish my mom and dad
could hear it.

—Sarah Murphy, *grade 2*

Lonely . . . to . . . "Cool Guy"

When I am lonely I feel like
an orphan in the orphan home and
all the other orphans are laughing
at me and they are saying that
I am a "dork" and no one
is playing with me. Perhaps
someday all the orphans
will stop laughing at me.
Someday someone will
come up to me and say:
"Do you want to play with me?"
Perhaps someday everybody
will call me "cool guy."

—Chris Zheng, *grade 2*

Not Fancy

I have a lion in me. He is fancy.

He thinks no one is better than him.

I have a lizard in me. He thinks

he's the best. I get so mad

I hit myself to try to get them out.

Neither of them are fancy.

Don't tell them I said that. I yell

at them: "You'd better come out

or I will get very angry."

So they came out and I had

to say what I had to say.

I told them "None of you are fancy!"

I'm still fast, so I kicked them and

they were never seen again.

—Brandon Stellato, *grade 2*

Lucas DiPietrantonio, *grade K*

Half Pegasus, Half Unicorn

I'm half Pegasus half
Unicorn

I never really want
to be around any
body. But I pretend to

just to be nice. I am
always sad, but I don't
know why. My horn

is full of power.
My wings make me
soar away.

I never let my real
self out. I wish I
could fly away.
My eyes are
as cold as the
sun. My fur is
as white as the
full moon. I
hope I never lose
my half Pegasus
half unicorn.

—Annick Marewski, *grade 3*

Miss Social Butterfly

I have a social butterfly in me. It has
the mouth of a motor that keeps
going and going. It flies around saying
hello to everyone and knows who they are.
It's loud and questioning, but it's pretty cool
to know everyone 'cause you get more friends
and you can annoy your parents.

—Natasha Davis, *grade 4*

—Nicole Battistoni *grade 3*

14

Sometimes I dream about
what the day would be like tomorrow.
Sometimes I think about
what I will look like
tomorrow. Like all dreams
you always find out sooner or later.
All I know is that I am a blue sky waiting
until the sun comes up. When the sun
does come up I see my shiny brown
hair and I see my eyes sparkling in
the sun. When I see my reflection in
the dark blue lake I notice my medium
skin and how it looks like the carpet in
my aunt's guest room. Good thing
tomorrow never dies so I can see
myself again.

—Maria Melfe, *grade 5*

—Maggie Selvin, *grade 4*

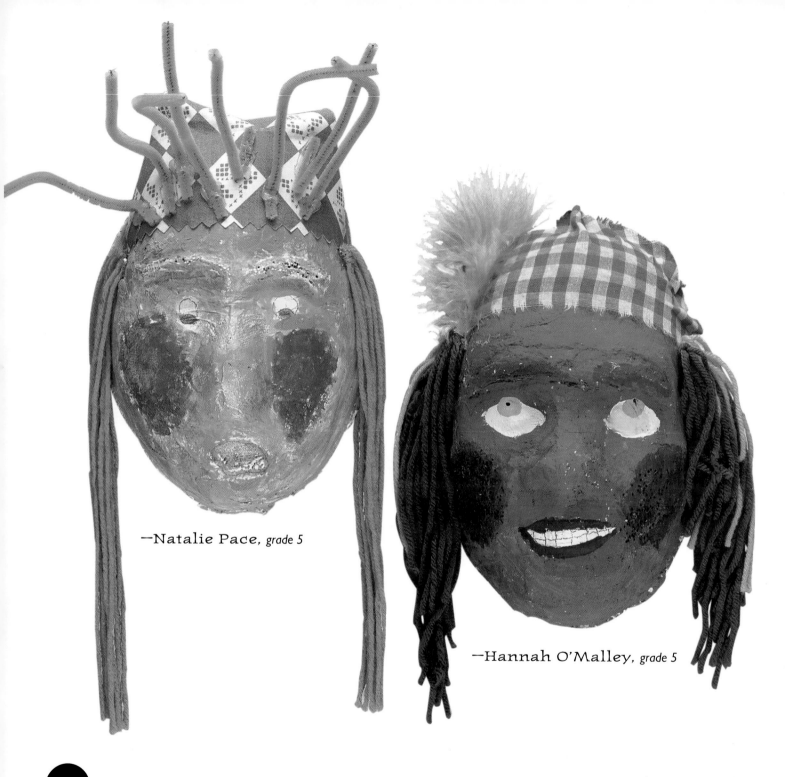

—Natalie Pace, *grade 5*

—Hannah O'Malley, *grade 5*

The Three Parts of Me

There are three parts of me. I am
      three different people.
In one mood, my hair is always down
and blows wild and free like a butterfly.
My eyes are gray storm clouds
      that never rain.
I never care about anything in this
      part of me.
My skin is light and rough like sandpaper
that has been used many times.

In my second mood, my hair is never
down, but up, swinging in the breeze,
      trying to get down.
My eyes are light blue sapphires,
polished until they shine with the strength
of a million stars. My skin is smooth.
If clouds had texture, that's what it would
feel like. In this mood, I have freckles
that sprinkle the tip of my nose
like small gold beads.

My last mood is my favorite. My hair
is half up, with the bottom flying in the wind.
This time, my eyes are green emeralds,
not so shiny this time. My skin is darker
like day turning to dusk.

I always wonder
how my day would have gone
if I had been a different
part of myself.

—Kristin Jordhamo, *grade 5*

17

I feel sad like a person

who has nothing—

like a guy I and my family

know who is trying to get

him a job so he can

have money so he can

get stuff.

—De'Jarah Cotton, *grade 2*

In My Only World

The most lost thing is me. It
is like a red room. In that room it is
just me and what I care about. If someone
talks to me I cannot hear them. I just stand
or sit and not move. It is like dead. I just think
and think what am I going to do next.
It is like my only world. Then all of a sudden
I am in my room and my mom just finished
her sentence and I ask her to repeat herself.
I wish my mom wouldn't ask me to do so
much stuff when I am in my only world.

—Shawn Tartaglione, *grade 4*

—William Nunn, *grade 3*

When people make fun of you
just because you're shy it hurts
like a broken heart.

—Quayron, *grade 4*

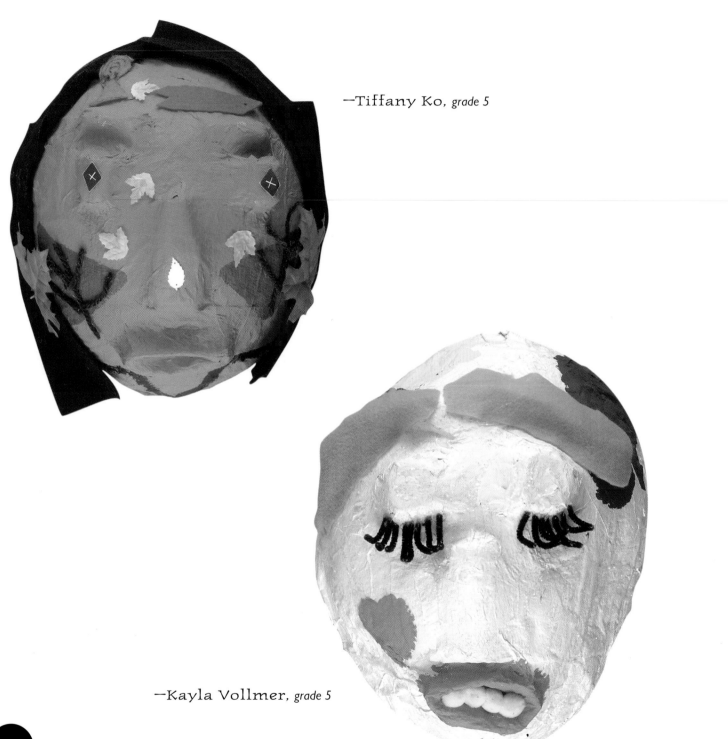

—Tiffany Ko, *grade 5*

—Kayla Vollmer, *grade 5*

20

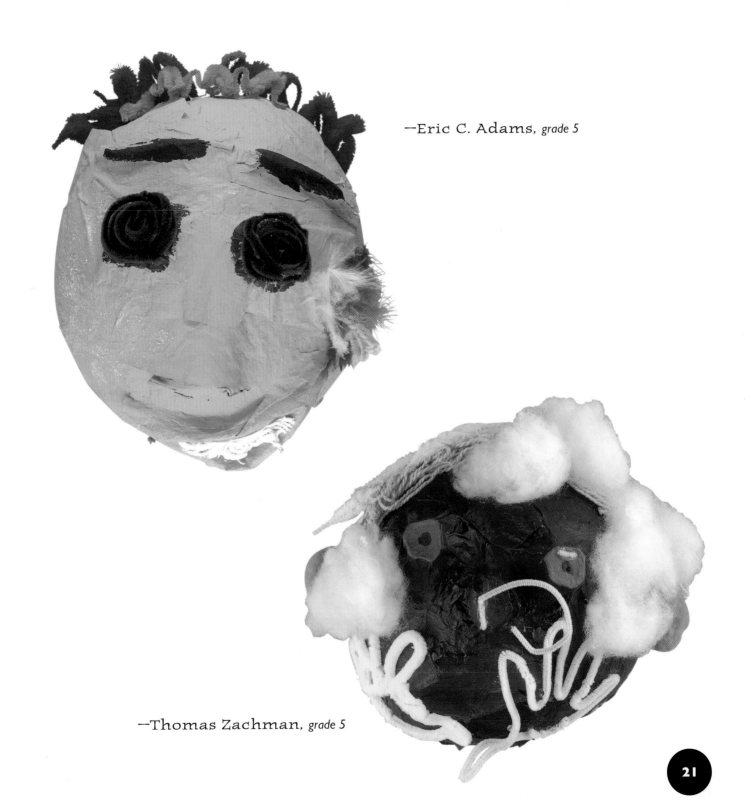

—Eric C. Adams, *grade 5*

—Thomas Zachman, *grade 5*

My Powerful Shield

My safest place in the world
is my bed. It's like a dome
at night where covers are like
a powerful shield protecting you
from terrible dreams.
It is like heaven
except you're floating
on a white steady covered pillow.
It's like you're royalty deciding
whether to dream or just
pleasantly snooze.
Maybe someday we can stay in bed
all day. Maybe we can all decide
to be royalty. Maybe we can
all float on pillows in heaven.
Until then
enjoy the moonlit night.

—Danielle Gobbo, *grade 5*

—Michelle Clarke, *grade 5*

Me . . . Someday

The most delicate thing is a ballet
dancer dancing across the stage in shiny
pink toe shoes. Doing turns and leaps so
gracefully that the wood in her shoes sounds
like the pitter patter of rain sparkling in the sun.
The dancer soars through the air landing so
soft she almost looks weightless.
The dancer rises to the tip of her toe on her
right foot doing a P-K arabesque and then
she does a torgetee. The audience is in
awe as they see her finish. As the dancer
receives flowers tears roll down her cheeks.
I wish I could be like that someday . . .
but that's what ballet class is for.

—Caitlin Tremblay, *grade 5*

—Jori Breite, *grade 1*

My Court

My place is the platform
by my driveway. There is
a basketball hoop there
and I bring a radio down
with me. There are a lot
of trees of all sizes around
it. I go down there to take out
my frustrations, to practice,
and listen to music. When
I'm down there I put everything
behind me and shoot around.

—Kyle Emigh, *grade 5*

Playing hockey is like
gliding on clouds when the
wind is blowing against your helmet
and then—KAPOW—you get
checked into the boards. It hurts.
But you don't want to be
a baby so you get up.

—Nick Sansone, *grade 5*

24

—Kevin White, *grade 4*

Warmth Spreads

I feel close to my warm bed
when I sit around a campfire
on a moist night. I see colors
of orange and red burning in my mind.
I taste the smore I am eating.
I smell smoke coming from the
fire. I hear crackling. Sparks fly into
the air. Warmth spreads into my body.

—Jonah Feitelson, *grade 2*

When I feel lonely I feel
like I'm sitting by the beach
at night while the moon
is shining by the water with
crystals in the breeze.
And then I close my eyes
and I feel like I'm flying
by the moonlight. And
then I feel like I want to
sit on the moonlight and
then I fall asleep.

—Natalie Strauss, *grade 2*

—Adriana, *grade 5*

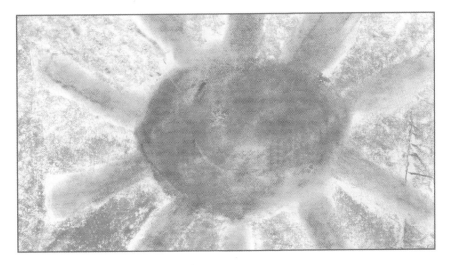

—Anna Drabek, *grade 5*

The Summer

It is the summer. The sun is beaming. It looks like a big lollipop. When I run in the fields with the flowers I drop and all the flowers are in my face and they tickle. They all look like people with yellow faces. They look like yellow circles.

—Olivia Bouffard, *grade 2*

—Connor Schafer, *grade K*

28

Dancing Clown

When I'm happy
I feel like a clown
dancing on water.

—Jared Warren, *grade 1*

—Kaylyn, *grade 1*

Art credits

Author index

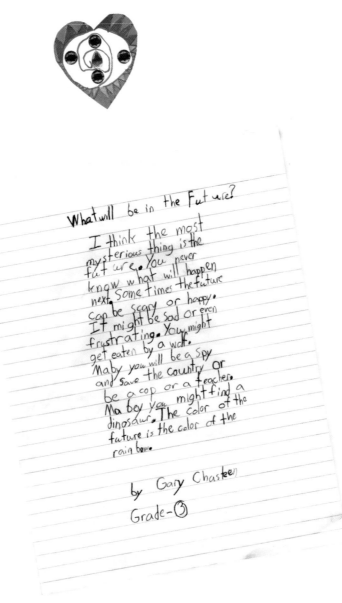

What will be in the Future?

I think the most
mysterious thing is the
future. You never
know what will happen
next. Sometimes the future
can be scary or happy.
It might be sad or even
frustrating. You might
get eaten by a wolf.
Maby you will be a spy
and save the country or
be a cop or a teacher.
Ma bey you might find a
dinosaur. The color of the
future is the color of the
rain bow.

by Gary Chasteen
Grade-3

Gary Chasteen, *grade 3*